Five Steps to a
Good Relationship

For Christian Singles

Reed Calaway

ISBN 979-8-88943-886-1 (paperback)
ISBN 979-8-88943-887-8 (digital)

Christian Faith Publishing
832 Park Avenue
Meadville, PA 16335
www.christianfaithpublishing.com

Printed in the United States of America

CONTENTS

INTRODUCTION

Some years ago, I was driving down the highway and saw a billboard that read, "We Feel in Love." I wasn't sure if I read it right, so I got off the next exit and came around to take another look. It was an advertisement for a dating service. The two people on the billboard looked excited about their relationship.

I thought to myself, "Love should be established on more than a feeling, because emotions are impulsive and unreliable." What happens if those feelings change after seeing things about the other person that they don't like?

Some personality traits take time to reveal themselves. What we thought was love in the beginning, may be an emotional endorphin rush we experienced before we got a closer look at that person.

Moving too fast will cause you to do foolish things, but hindsight is twenty-twenty. Seeing that billboard was the beginning of many formal and informal teachings I began to do on relationships and marriage leading up to the writing of this book.

The importance of the five steps

There's been an increase in dating services, social media connections, and reality shows about relationships. Their popularity suggests that people are looking for the right person but are having a hard time finding them.

Not knowing what to look for causes difficulty in navigating new relationships. It can discourage you from connecting with the person who may be right for you. The five steps in this book will help you avoid the disappointments and the emotional hurt that come with bad bonding and relationships that are going nowhere.

The steps given in this book will help you apply practical wisdom in making choices, by providing you with good instruction and biblical principles. You'll be able to adjust how you connect with a love interest going forward, and make the right choices while evaluating your past relationships. The five steps will challenge you to look carefully at your present relationship and identify what you're doing right, and what you may be doing wrong.

Read the book with a friend and decide what you want in a relationship. Stay true to yourself and don't compromise. Share what you learn with others because someone may need to hear what you have to say.

> And do not be conformed to this world [any longer with its superficial values and customs], but be transformed *and* progressively changed [as you mature spiritually] by the renewing of your mind, [focusing on godly values and ethical attitudes], so that you may prove [for yourselves] what the will of God is, that which is good and acceptable and perfect [in His plan and purpose for you]. (Romans 12:2 AMP)

CHAPTER 1

Starting from the Beginning

Then God blessed them, and God said to them, "Be fruitful and multiply; fill the earth and subdue it; have dominion over the fish of the sea, over the birds of the air, and over every living thing that moves on the earth."
—Genesis 1:28 NKJV

A perfect world

Consider a world where every man and woman were as genetically perfect and physically beautiful as the next. If you lived in that type of world, how would you select your partner, and by what standard would you choose them?

Can you imagine having no concern for deteriorating age, illness, clothing, or shelter? The first man and woman lived in that type of world and were created in the image and likeness of God. They were His physical representation on earth, and shared equally in power and dominion. They were perfect for each other.

God's plan for the man and woman was, and is, to be fruitful and multiply and fill the earth with people. But Adam was the first man created, and the only one of his kind, and couldn't accomplish it alone. Adam had no knowledge of woman because his only desire was for a relationship with his Creator, therefore, the desire for companionship had to be aroused in him.

Genesis 2:18–22 (AMP) tells us,

> Now the Lord God said, "It is not good (beneficial) for the man to be alone; I will make him a helper [one who balances him—a counterpart who is suitable and complementary for him." So the Lord God formed out of the ground every animal of the field and every bird of the air, and brought them to Adam to see what he would call them; and whatever the man called a living creature, that was its name. And the man gave names to all the livestock, and to the birds of the air, and to every animal of the field; but for Adam there was not found a helper [that was] suitable (a companion) for him. So the Lord God caused a deep sleep to fall upon Adam; and while he slept, he took one of his ribs and closed up the flesh at that place. And the rib which the Lord God had taken from the man he made (fashioned, formed) into a woman, and he brought her and presented her to the man.

As Adam observed the coupling of all the creatures God created, he also began to long for a companion. The Bible doesn't tell us how long Adam was on earth before God decided it was time to create the woman, but we do know that she was always in God's plan.

The Bible tells us that God put Adam into a deep sleep and created the woman, but it doesn't tell us how long the woman was with God before she was brought to the man. It's my opinion that God wouldn't create the woman and not give her an understanding of who she was created to be, and her purpose on earth.

Genesis 2:23–25 (AMP) tells us what Adam said when the woman was brought to him:

> This is now bone of my bones,
> And flesh of my flesh;
> She shall be called Woman,
> Because she was taken out of Man.
>
> For this reason a man shall leave his father and his mother, and shall be joined to his wife; and they shall become one flesh. And the man and his wife were both naked and were not ashamed or embarrassed.

The woman was perfect for accomplishing God's plan on earth with the man. She was a helper and partner in rulership; she balanced him and was a counterpart that was suitable, and a complement to who he was. The man and woman were equal in rank and dominion, and there was no power struggle, or need for dominance over the other. They were one, and lived in harmony with God, creation, and each other.

Becoming one flesh

The first marriage ceremony was performed by God, and it is universally recognized in all cultures. The Bible tells us that the rib the Lord God took from the man, he made into a woman, and brought and presented her to the man.

Up until this very day, it's a tradition that fathers walk their daughters down the aisle to present her to the man, and she takes his name. They become one flesh by a blood covenant cut between them on their wedding night. That covenant is consummated by the mingling of their blood in a sexual union.

There are cultures that assign a person to retrieve the blood-stained bedsheets on the wedding night and display them as proof that the marriage was consummated. The bloodstained sheets show the pureness of the bride, and if the sheets aren't bloodstained, and the bride was found to be sexually impure because she'd already been with a man, the groom could reject her.

Even in traditional western ceremonies, the bride wears white as a sign of her purity, and if the marriage isn't consummated, it can be annulled.

Soul ties

A marriage is consummated by a husband and wife through becoming one flesh in a sexual union. But becoming one flesh is more than uniting two bodies. Sex is a spiritual union consummated by a physical act.

The physical act of joining your body with someone, brings you together as one, by mingling your blood with theirs, and a spiritual union takes place as you bond emotionally and mentally through that experience. God designed the joining of a man and woman to work through sexual intimacy when engaging in sexual intercourse, and it causes an emotional and mental bond called a "soul tie." Soul ties tether two people together emotionally and mentally, because the mind and emotions belong to the spirit, and when a man and woman engage in sex, they aren't only dealing with the physical part of a person; they're dealing with their "inward man," the soul. This is why so many people find it hard to end a relationship after they've been sexually active with someone for a while.

Sex was designed for two people to become one through marriage, which is supposed to be a permanent condition and not a temporary situation. Even when an unmarried couple know the relationship isn't good, it's difficult to leave after they develop a soul tie.

Sex isn't a man idea; it's a God idea, and He's the author of relationships. If anyone knows how it's supposed to work, it's Him. Sex is designed to bring a relationship between the husband and wife to a deeper level. Afterward, and every time they come together, it confirms and reaffirms their relationship.

Soul ties were designed by God to benefit a marriage by creating closeness, familiarity, and sincere concern for one another. Soul ties add strength and adhesiveness to a relationship, and work toward emotional stability and continuity that strengthens with time. If the couple have children, their souls will be tied to their children, who are the fruit of that union. But when a man or woman operate outside of God's purpose for a sexual union, soul ties become destructive and emotionally damaging.

The intimacy of the marriage covenant is intended to be enjoyed by a lasting relationship because sexual intimacy will create a soul tie whether two people are married or not. Indulging in sex outside of the marriage is transgressing God's purpose for intimacy between a husband and wife.

Sin complicates things

1 Corinthians 6:16–20 (MSG) says,

> There's more to sex than mere skin on skin. Sex is as much spiritual mystery as physical fact. As written in Scripture, "The two become one." Since we want to become spiritually one with the Master, we must not pursue the kind of sex that avoids commitment and intimacy, leaving us more lonely than ever—the kind of sex that can never "become one." There is a sense in which sexual sins are different from all others. In sexual sin we violate the sacredness of our own bodies, these bodies that were made for God-given and God-modeled love, for "becoming one" with

another. Or didn't you realize that your body is a
sacred place, the place of the Holy Spirit? Don't
you see that you can't live however you please,
squandering what God paid such a high price
for? The physical part of you is not some piece of
property belonging to the spiritual part of you.
God owns the whole works. So let people see
God in and through your body.

The sins we commit are through our body, but in sexual sins,
we cause our body to cooperate by joining in sin with another person's body. There are paternity tests, blood tests, and even DNA results that prove that people joined their body with someone in a sexual union. Therefore, it shouldn't surprise you that through sexual intercourse, you become "one flesh" in your sin with someone else.

In 1 Corinthians 6:18 (AMP), it says, "Run away from sexual immorality [in any form, whether thought or behavior, whether visual or written]. Every other sin that a man commits is outside the body, but the one who is sexually immoral sins against his own body."

Soul ties weren't designed to impact you negatively, but when you operate outside of God's plan for sex, you expose yourself to emotional fragmentation that divides. This fragmentation causes estrangements that work contrary to the adhesiveness and emotional stability that occur when someone is a permanent part of your life. But if they leave, a piece of that person remains with you, and a part of you goes with that person. That doesn't change even if you bond with someone new.

Did you ever hear someone say, "I love them both, but not in the same way." They are emotionally fragmented, and instead of a godly soul tie, an ungodly soul tie developed, and that space is occupied by someone who's no longer a part of their life.

Your body wasn't created only for sexual gratification, but the real intimacy of a marriage covenant. When you use your body to gratify a lust and think you can just walk away, there are consequences. The more sexual contacts you have outside of marriage, determines the amount of sexual baggage you'll carry into a marriage.

But how did we get so far away from God's original plan for the man and woman? Again, sin complicates things.

In Genesis chapter 3, we have the account of the woman and man's transgression and how it changed their relationship with God and each other, and also how it affects us today. Genesis chapter 5 verse 2 tells us that God called them "both" Adam on the day they were created. They were one in God's eyes, but after the transgression in the garden, Adam called his wife Eve.

Who you identify with gives you purpose and will establish your identity. God created the man and woman in His image and likeness, and they identified with Him; thus, they had their purpose.

The man and woman ruled as gods in the world He gave them and had the ability to create life, which was an important part of fulfilling God's plan on earth. Through the man and woman, the families, societies, nations, and generations of the world came into existence. When you know who you are, your purpose directs your life. But after the fall, everything would change.

Falling out of fellowship

In the beginning, God was the source of the man and woman's life, identity, and purpose, but they fell out of right fellowship with Him. After they sinned, they began to identify with their fallen nature, and not with God. They were no longer motivated by the life of God that once worked in them, but by the sin nature working through them. They were no longer God-conscious, but self-conscious. They became earth-centric rather than heavenly-minded. Once they lost their identity, their purpose changed, and they were who they became rather than who they were.

The man and woman's disobedience affected every generation down through the ages to this very day, and at this point in time, we are in constant pursuit of identity and purpose.

Who and what you identify with gives you your purpose. If it's a career, you'll find your purpose in that. If it's in the family, they'll give you your sense of identity and purpose. If it's your friends, that's who'll determine your identity, and in them you'll find your purpose.

Who or what you identify with gives you purpose, and the loss of it causes your self-worth to be broken. We determine our self-worth by identity and purpose.

A change in desire

God's standard for a man and woman was equality. However, God knew that after the transgression, men and women would struggle with that. So God set the disorder of sin in order according to His pattern of creation.

The man was created first, and the woman was created for the man as helper and companion. She was taken out of man as someone who would complement him; therefore, God said to the woman,

> I will greatly multiply
> Your pain in childbirth;
> In pain you will give birth to children;
> Yet your desire and longing will be for your
>   husband,
> And he will rule [with authority] over you and
>   be responsible for you. (Genesis 3:16 AMP)

That portion of scripture makes me believe that all the children born before the fall were painless births. And next, there's an age-old misconception that God's will was that one sex would dominate the other, and some men interpret the word *rule* to mean male dominance.

The word *rule* was speaking to the role the man would have over the woman in a marriage covenant. Sin separated the woman's relationship with God, and now her desire would be for her husband, which gave him power to rule over her. You can see that today with women who set aside their relationship with Christ to pursue a man.

But if a woman doesn't want the man, he has nothing to control her with.

As generations passed, and men moved farther away from God and each other, they began to exercise dominance over one another. Women, who are physically weaker, lost their place and voice.

Even though the women were placed under subjection to men because men are physically stronger, they were covered by their husbands if they were married, and the husbands were responsible for their care.

Adam, on the other hand, was dealt with by God according to provision because that would become his primary purpose, and he would gain identity through his responsibility to his wife and family. To this very day, men feel a sense of shame if they can't provide for them.

As for the serpent, which is the devil and Satan, God said,

> And I will put enmity (open hostility)
> Between you and the woman,
> And between your seed (offspring) and her Seed;
> He shall [fatally] bruise your head,
> And you shall [only] bruise His heel. (Genesis
> 3:15 AMP)

That was the first prophetic word concerning the redemptive work of Jesus Christ who would be the Savior of all men. From that point on, Adam began to call his wife's name Eve, which means the "Mother of all living."

The sin in the garden caused all men to die, but through the seed of the woman, all men will be made alive. Satan would try to corrupt, hinder, or stop that seed from being birthed because every man born into the world from then on would be the potential hope of God's salvation for all mankind.

As men began to multiply on earth, who someone chose as their partner was their own responsibility, but God hasn't changed His mind about being fruitful and multiplying, even though we have.

Satan has done such a good job that sexually active young men and women view pregnancy as an inconvenience and children as a burden. Being a father or mother has become a hindrance to their future plans, and the fruit of the womb is rejected for pleasure.

We'd rather fulfill our sensual appetites than please God, and we avoid unwanted pregnancies with birth control, contraceptives, condoms, vasectomies, morning-after pills, and abortions.

Psalm 127:3–5 (AMP) says,

> Behold, children are a heritage *and gift* from the
> Lord,
> The fruit of the womb a reward.
> Like arrows in the hand of a warrior,
> So are the children of one's youth.
> How blessed [happy and fortunate] is the man
> whose quiver is filled with them.

Today, men and women seek sexual pleasure instead of pleasing God. Being fruitful and multiplying is no longer their pursuit, and God's plan to produce the peoples, societies, and nations of the world is no longer a service for God, but about self-gratification.

Young men of past and present generations are forgetting they carry the seeds of life in their loins until some young woman gets pregnant. Likewise, young women don't want to acknowledge that children are waiting to be birthed into the world through them, and avoid getting pregnant.

There are financial institutions called banks that we deposit our wealth into as security for our future, but the most precious commodity in this world are souls. It shouldn't surprise you that someone would think of creating "sperm banks" for men to deposit their wealth into. But for those who would teach that sex is only for procreation, that issue should be addressed.

The Bible teaches that sexual intimacy was given to the man and woman for procreation. Remember that God told them to be fruitful and multiply. But also take in to account that God formed pleasure centers in the male and female anatomy so that being fruitful was enjoyable, and multiplying was the result.

Sex was created for the man and woman to have as often as they pleased, and the Apostle Paul writes to the church in Corinth about that same subject.

> Now as to the matters of which you wrote: It is good (beneficial, advantageous) for a man not to touch a woman [outside marriage]. But because of [the temptation to participate in] sexual immorality, let each man have his own wife, and let each woman have her own husband. The husband must fulfill his [marital] duty to his wife [with good will and kindness], and likewise the wife to her husband. The wife does not have [exclusive] authority over her own body, but the husband shares with her; and likewise the husband does not have [exclusive] authority over his body, but the wife shares with him. Do not deprive each other [of marital rights], except perhaps by mutual consent for a time, so that you may devote yourselves [unhindered] to prayer, but come together again so that Satan will not tempt you [to sin] because of your lack of self-control. (1 Corinthians 7:1–5 AMP)

CHAPTER 2

Love or Lust

A flood cannot put out love.
Rivers cannot drown love.
Would people despise a man for giving
everything he owns for love?
—Song of Solomon 8:7–9 ERV

A young man stood in line, waiting to give his order to the barista, and observed a girl picking up her order. When he returned to his friends, he informed them that he was in love and directed their attention toward the young woman. His friends laughed at that idea and said, "You're suffering from a case of lust. You don't even know who she is." What he never noticed was that the girl's friends were watching him checking her out because women are more observant than men.

Job, in response to his friends suggesting that his calamities may be because of some sexual misconduct, said, "I made a covenant with mine eyes not to look lustfully at a young woman" (Job 31:1 NIV).

Job understood the connection between seeing and thinking and how your thoughts determine what you see. Allowing someone's physical appearance to be your primary attraction will never bring you to a meeting of the minds because the brain is in the head, and there has to be more than a physical attraction in order for a real relationship to develop.

Your eyes are controlled by your thoughts, and will center on what attracts you most. There are people who are into eyes, and others into lips, and some give attention to teeth. For some, it may be hair, legs, or breast. But whether it's abs, triceps, biceps, or the gluteus maximus, whatever attracts you is what you'll give the most attention to when observing someone of the opposite sex.

Four types of love

There are four types of love expressed in the Greek language. There's the God kind of love called agape. There's also the love for mother, father, siblings, and close relatives, called *storge*. There is also *phileo*, which is where we get the word *philanthropist*. The last and least of them all is eros, which is a sensual passionate type of love, that if left unchecked, can influence and dominate the other three.

Vine's Expository Dictionary of Biblical Words explains agape, which is the God kind of love, as the characteristic of Christianity. It's the type of love that was previously unknown until revealed by the Spirit of revelation.

Agape love is God's will concerning an attitude we should have toward one another. It's not the love of complacency or affection; it's an act of the will and a deliberate choice.

Christlike love, whether exercised toward the brethren or men generally, is not an impulse from the feelings and doesn't always run with our natural inclinations. It doesn't spend itself only on those for whom some affinity is discovered.

Agape love is the type of love that God has for the world, Christ has for the church, and husbands should have for their wives. It transcends physical attraction, sexual gratification, and any emotional impulses you may feel. It's a choice you make and a commitment that you keep.

Agape love is foreign to our fallen nature because it can only be attained through the operation of the Holy Spirit.

Storge is the type of love that comes out of a natural connection with people of our own bloodline. It's the special love shared between parents, children, and relatives. Phileo love is friendly, affectionate, and socially motivated. Again, the word *philanthropist*, which is a person who contributes to the welfare of others by giving to good causes comes from the word *phileo*.

Phileo love shows loyalty to family, friends, and community. It strengthens the bonds that contribute to healthy joining when applied to male-female relationships. Storge and phileo have their origins in agape, which gives them godly qualities that make them operate in a beneficial way for anyone exercising them.

Separate and apart from agape love, storge love becomes exclusive and gives little attention to people outside of the family. Phileo love, apart from agape, ignores the needs of some while showing preference for others. Phileo love can be self-serving and self-righteous when it's not Christ-centered.

Eros

Eros love has its origins in Greek mythology. Dictionaries that define love as an intense feeling of deep affection and passion are defining eros. Those definitions are familiar to us because we associate them with love, and eros is the basis for most of what we call love today.

In Greek mythology, Eros is the god of passion and sex, who is the son of Aphrodite, the goddess of love and beauty. Aphrodite also had a son named Hermaphroditus, who was said to be a beautiful boy and the god of hermaphrodites and androgynous people.

Eros also has a Roman counterpart named Cupid, who is the god of romance and desire. Cupid is the son of Venus the goddess of love, who is Aphrodite's Hellenistic counterpart.

Pictures of naked babies with wings, shooting arrows of passion into the hearts of men and women, are inspired by mythical stories of Cupid. Those images have become the symbol of Valentine's Day, but like Eros, Cupid's love is impulsive, emotional, and driven by the sensuality that provoke feelings of never-ending passion.

The Greek god of mythology Eros is the reason so many women and men have the wrong idea of true love and suffer unfulfilled expectations.

Shouldn't we be passionate?

Passion is good in its proper place and timing, but you can't sustain a certain level of passion without it losing strength. A healthy relationship is more than how you feel in the moment, and you may not always feel passionate. Once you settle into learning about your partner, you'll have to deal with their character issues as well as yours, and that may not be so romantic.

Passionate love draws its satisfaction from an intense physical chemistry that will fade, and afterward, you're dealing with the practical side of your relationship. Passionate love has to mature into something sustainable to be real. The love that generates from eros reveals how we're guided by our feelings rather than our reason.

Guarding your heart

Proverbs 4:23 (NIV) says, "Above all else, guard your heart, for everything you do flows from it."

Your heart represents the center of your being, and like a gatekeeper, you should guard the place of your affections by setting boundaries on how far you'll allow your desires to roam. Exercising emotional restraint will enable you to take authority over how fast you'll invest in a relationship.

Ungodly soul ties form when you get intimately involved with someone before you know them socially and become emotionally tied to a stranger. Proverbs 4:23 says, "Guard your heart"; it doesn't say, "Follow your heart!"

Soul ties are emotional and psychological entanglements that tether two people together. Once a soul tie is formed it's hard to break, and can remain in place regardless of how much time or distance there is between two people, because thoughts and feelings aren't bound by time or distance. Like a time traveler, you can revisit the past over and over again in your mind.

Married couples form godly soul ties, but people operating outside of a marriage covenant form ungodly soul ties. There are people who have moved on with their life, got married, and have children, but have their souls tied to a past lover. If their marriage fails, they'll look for that person on different social media outlets, and even go as far as returning to the town or city they left to reconnect with that person.

Losing your mind

Did you ever hear someone ask, "Are you losing your mind?" They usually ask that question when someone is acting unreasonable or is out of control. Losing your mind is what happens when a person is controlled by their emotions and allows them to overrule their reason and intellect. They've literally lost control of their mind!

Emotions aren't supposed to guide us, because emotions don't have intellect or reason; they just feel. You should be guided by good judgment in your decision-making because anyone controlled by their feelings is out of control.

Emotions are indicators that gauge what we feel in relation to our experiences, whether the experience we feel is good or bad. That information is passed on to our reason and intellect for processing. Finally, the "will," where a decision is made concerning "I will," or "I will not," is made.

When our emotions are in control, the intellect and reason, along with the will, lose their ability to do what they were designed for. When emotions take over, the intellect, reason, and will come under its authority.

Breaking ungodly soul ties

When you don't recognize the emotional and psychological effects of your actions, the consequences will still be the same. Using your body in a way that it wasn't created to be used will cause you to develop ungodly soul ties, and you can find yourself tethered to someone in your past, and it will be hard to move forward.

Have you ever considered why there's so much emotional trauma when you break up with someone whom you've been with for a long time, even though you know it was the right thing to do? You've bonded emotionally and psychologically with that person, and the longer you stay, the harder the breakup, and there's fragmentation.

Your relationship wasn't meant to be a temporary experience but a permanent condition, because God created sex and relationships to work a specific way. Two souls are bound together through a sexual union in the relationship, and it works that way whether done correctly or incorrectly.

There are men and women who spend their lives soul tied to someone, and they have no understanding of what happened to them. You can't just lie down, get up, and walk away without any consequences. Sex isn't a game, and relationships are serious; and you'll be affected even if you don't know what's happening to you.

Repentance

Repentance is a word that strikes a sour chord in many of us. Telling someone to repent is an accusation that a person is doing something that they need to stop doing, and people living in sin don't want to hear that. But sexual sins are called fornication, and that's a spiritual matter; therefore, it's important to deal with the spiritual aspect of a soul tie first.

Anyone with an ungodly soul tie needs to repent and ask God for forgiveness. Consider how easy it was to get sexually involved and move on without a second thought because restraint wasn't in your thinking. The conviction of the Holy Spirit became an ineffective voice in your conscience, and finally, you found yourself in love with someone who provided no fulfillment in your life.

You want your soul back, but unless you repent and get it right with God, you'll continue to be in bondage to the emotions that tethered you to that person.

God didn't create you to operate outside of His purpose for relationships, and the spiritual side of sex that ties two souls together has to be broken to get free. You have to deal with the spiritual nature of a soul tie before you can be free from its effect. Begin by acknowledging your sin, and repent.

Trying to break an ungodly soul tie in your own strength shows an ignorance of the spiritual nature of a soul tie. You're unconsciously carrying emotional baggage that takes a spiritual authority to correct because a spiritual boundary has been violated. But God will help you get free if you'll repent and ask Him to forgive you.

Forgiveness

Forgiveness means to "send away"; therefore, whatever you hold onto holds onto you, and unforgiveness becomes your jailer.

When you realize that forgiveness is an act of your will and not about how you feel, your decision to forgive will cause your feelings to catch up.

There are men and women who have soul ties because of their unforgiveness. Years have passed, and they remain stuck in time, while the other person has moved on. They haven't learned how to release and send away the bitterness and anger and desire for revenge that holds their heart captive. The mental and emotional energy used to think about that person keeps them bound because unforgiveness makes it impossible to get free. As I said before, "Whatever you hold onto holds onto you." You must forgive if you want God to forgive you.

Harboring resentment makes you a prisoner to the bitterness you feel toward that person. Unforgiveness strengthens a soul tie, but forgiveness benefits the person harboring those emotions, not the person who treated them unfairly even if the other person doesn't care.

A mental disconnection

Breaking an ungodly soul tie is our responsibility by an act of our will. God won't make you do anything you aren't willing to do because we are free-will agents.

Once you've repented and asked God for forgiveness, it's time to put your intellect, reason, and will back in its proper place. Your emotions have been in control up until this point, and they need to be brought back under control to make that mental disconnection.

Make up your mind that you're leaving the relationship and you're not going back. Make the decision to break that emotional entanglement that tethered you psychologically to that person in the first place. But telling yourself you need to move on won't work unless you've made up your mind.

Be willing to get rid of or give away any jewelry, gifts, or anything that can become mementos. Pictures are also reminders of experiences you shared together that will keep you emotionally connected.

All those types of things hold great emotional value in your heart and mind, and how hard it is to let them go will determine how hard it's going to be to get yourself free.

Music is also a powerful trigger; therefore, listening to sentimental music that reminds you of that person will evoke deep emotional feelings. It's important to remember that you're fighting to get your soul back, and God did His part; and now it's time to do yours. Again, you can measure the strength of your soul tie by how hard it is to get free.

A physical disconnection

A physical disconnection also has to take place. Distancing yourself physically from that person is for your own mental health. You need time and space to get yourself together; therefore, don't make any physical contact.

Touching, hugging, or kissing is more than casual because they convey messages according to how they're done. Kissing is a personal exercise in intimacy and a prelude to sex called foreplay. There's as much emotional and intimate information communicated through a kiss as having sex.

Sexual intimacy confirms and reaffirms a relationship and will cause it to continue. Sex reestablishes a soul tie; and if you're getting free, don't get entangled again by continuing a physical connection.

A social disconnection

The last step in breaking an ungodly soul tie is a social disconnection. You've physically disconnected from this person, and now you should stop all communications. Don't make contact by cell or text. Don't send or receive letters. Don't meet to talk because that puts you back in risk of physical contact. Don't allow third parties to be liaisons between you.

Communication is a relationship builder, and a conversation can reignite a fire that should be put out. Avoid places and events you shared together, and don't go on social media for updates on that person. Get off social media altogether for a while because friends you have in common will keep you updated and informed. It may take time, but you should be willing to do what's necessary to get free.

Remember that this person isn't a part of your life any longer, and you won't die because of it. You're fighting to get your soul back; therefore, guard your heart because it directs the course of your life.

CHAPTER 3

The Hookup Culture

*I beseech you therefore brethren, by the mercies of God, that ye present
your bodies a living sacrifice, holy, acceptable unto God, which is
your reasonable service. And be not conformed to this world, but
be ye transformed by the renewing of your mind, that ye may prove
what is that good, and acceptable, and perfect, will of God.*
—Romans 12:1–2 KJV

They met at a pool party, and the sexual attraction between them was so obvious that it didn't surprise anyone when they left together. The sex was great, but making conversation was difficult because they were sexually compatible, but socially incompatible; and after sex, there was nothing to talk about or do.

He was into fast cars and racing, and whenever they were with his friends, that's what they talked about. Watching cars go around in circles was ridiculous to her because she was into romantic movies, quiet evenings, and her book club. Those were the things she enjoyed; and when she was with her friends, that was their conversation, which for him was like being tied to a chair and tortured. So whenever her friends came around, he would leave. They had nothing in common but sex, so they decided to see each other occasionally for a hookup.

Casual sex, one-night stands, and no commitments

Everything you shouldn't do is what they do in the hookup culture. Brief encounters, casual sex, and one-night stands with no commitments, are characteristics of that culture, and are acceptable behavior. But our God-given inherent nature is to bond with the person we're intimate with.

When there's not a genuine connection with someone you're sexually involved with, it's a learned behavior and something practiced by those in that lifestyle, and men and women in the hookup culture have that mentality.

Fulfilling your own lust at the expense of another, or satisfying your sexual appetite by using someone, should be unacceptable behavior in any situation. But ignorance and bad character are overlooked for physical beauty, and sexual gratification takes the place of a genuine connection. That's how each new encounter is graded in a hookup culture.

Every partner is graded by who kisses better, how they perform in bed, and what sexual acts they will or will not do. The long-term consequence of that is, when they finally find someone whom they really want to be with, that person is unknowingly competing with all the previous lovers their partner has had.

The more sexual encounters a person has, the harder it is to be satisfied with one person. If they don't measure up to your expectations according to previous experiences, you'll continue to search for that superwoman if you're a man, and that superman if you're a woman.

Serial dating

Serial daters avoid monogamous relationships and are usually involved with two or more people at the same time. They stay away from relationships that limit their activity because why should they be with one person when there are so many available people out there?

Each new encounter is approached like a conquest, because they're not looking for the right one; that's not how they think. It's about playing the field, therefore a relationship with a serial dater has little chance of developing into anything lasting.

Sexual activity without commitment sabotages developing relationships because the connections that encourage genuine bonding loses value when there's no desire for permanence. Again, emotional disconnections are learned practices and not the way we were created.

Sexual orientation

The way a person is sexually orientated will determine how they approach sex and male-female relationships. Young boys who are encouraged to get sexually active at a young age by their peers view sex as a physical experience, and nothing more. This causes them to see girls as sexual objects, and sexual activity as a "rite of passage."

These young men gain acceptance by their peers once they become sexually active, but it also shapes the way they approach the opposite sex going forward. They have a hard time seeing females as people with intelligence and personality, and not just bodies.

Girls in that same situation learn from their peers how to use sexual attraction to manipulate boys. This creates problems for them in the future if they don't mature out of using sexuality in their social activities with the opposite sex.

All of their encounters with males will begin on a sexual level, and because females are naturally more socially engaging than males, they'll use sexual appeal to interact socially. This causes the lines between a genuine connection and a sexual connection to get blurred.

If you haven't noticed, our society is built on sexuality, and some women won't leave their house without having their game face on.

Young Christian men and women are tempted to go along with the norms of their peer groups when people with different values are their influencers. Their Christian beliefs get challenged, and out of fear of rejection, their personal morals and Christian values are compromised.

The type of Christians that join themselves to worldly norms and begin to do whatever a certain group is doing, depart from what they've been taught, and embrace the ideas and beliefs of this world.

Ephesians 5:11–12 (AMP) says, "Do not participate in the worthless *and* unproductive deeds of darkness, but instead expose them [by exemplifying personal integrity, moral courage, and godly character]; for it is disgraceful even to mention the things that such people practice in secret."

Abstinence

A person that's abstinent because of a religious or moral stand doesn't fit into the hookup culture. Young men and women in that culture believe that sex isn't a big thing, and anyone who isn't doing it is sad. But the person who saves themselves for marriage doesn't have a history of sexual partners to compare their husband or wife with, and as far as they know, their partner is perfect for them.

A virgin may be out of step with everyone in that culture, but what they're missing out on is soul ties, STDs, and unwanted pregnancy. The statistics that I researched said an estimated 374 million new infections are reported each year. I'm sure that number has increased by now, and how many unreported cases are out there waiting to connect with someone?

Social dynamics of the hookup culture

The social dynamics in the hookup culture for males and females alike are confusing for anyone who wants to live by sound moral values. There aren't any rules in a hookup culture, and there's no place for someone who wants to conduct themselves in an appropriate manner unless they compromise.

Young men who treat females as sexual objects make up the masculine side of the culture. And the young women who use sexual influence to manipulate men are on the other side. In between the two, there's everything else.

Both sides put themselves out there by posting suggestive pictures on social media that emphasize what they believe are their most attractive physical attributes. The females don't understand why they can't find a real relationship, and why men want to go right to bed. And the males who know the game play it to the max.

Meanwhile, in real time, young women are doing a balancing act between what is appropriate and what may be too over-the-top when preparing for a night out. They know that if someone's looking for a hookup, they'll interpret friendliness as availability and sexy attire as accessibility. So she doesn't want to send the wrong message.

The thinking behind looking presentable is an opportunity to make a positive connection if it presents itself, which is the motivation for looking the best she can. She's also aware that she's competing with other girls, so looking good is a part of her appeal for social engagement, not necessarily about a sexual encounter. But if she's hanging in the wrong places, she may get the opposite of what she wants.

Misinterpreting interpretations

Women are naturally social creatures and would like to enjoy themselves without getting sexually harassed when out with friends having fun. The male with a correct social IQ understands that, and knows genuine friendliness and sincere social availability are attractive to a woman. That's a lesson that many young men with low social IQs have to learn.

When meeting someone individually or in groups, the ability to accurately assess your social atmosphere and people works to your advantage. But a person with poor social skills doesn't pick up on subtle nonverbal cues from people in their surroundings.

A low social IQ will cause body language and facial expressions to be ignored, and the sexually motivated male wants to believe that all the girls in the room are available. He can't read the room, so he becomes the obnoxious person whom everyone avoids.

Women who don't want to be approached shift their body position in a direction that doesn't line up with an approaching male. She also avoids eye contact and won't return smiles. But if she's interested, she'll make appropriate eye contact and appear friendly so that the male will see she's approachable.

The sexually motivated male doesn't get that and will come at a female suddenly without assessing the situation.

The flirt

Any young man who's been in the hookup game for a while is familiar with certain personality types. A culture that's about the hookup is a perfect playground for the flirt personality. Men who consider themselves players get played by the flirt, and afterward, feel like amateurs.

She plays their game, but without the payout. And when they realize what's going on, it's too late because they're overcommitted. Young men, that can't control their sexual drives, give the flirt everything she needs to control them.

Foolish men are her toys, and the flirt will use her sexual appeal to manipulate them. For her, it's only amusement because the truth is, she doesn't want them; she's just having fun.

A flirt will ignore the social nuances that apply to appropriate male-female interactions. She invades a man's personal space, which is a suggestion of sexual interest. She's good at playing "eye games," and she'll bait a man with an inviting smile to lure him into her net.

A sexually motivated male will spend his time and money chasing something he's not going to get, and when she gets bored, she'll move on to someone else, leaving him embarrassed and bewildered. Men who have had past dealings with flirts feel like idiots, and afterward, they call them ugly names.

One of the most toxic relationships that can happen is a jealous person with a flirt. That type of relationship can cause violence between two men and also to her. An unsuspecting male may never know she's with someone because of the way she conducts herself. The person who's in the relationship with her may feel disrespected and react, or can remain silent and embarrassed. A flirt and a jealous person make a toxic relationship.

James 1:14 (KJV) says, "But every man is tempted, when he is drawn away of his own lust, and enticed."

Friends with benefits

A friend is someone with whom you share a mutual bond of trust and care for outside of a sexual relationship. If a person is a true friend, there won't be a desire to cross an unspoken boundary that leads to sex.

Friendships are established on something different than an underlying sexual attraction, because sex is reserved for someone who holds a particular place in your life that's more than a friend. But it's also common for two people that start out as friends to end up together, because there was a mutual attraction from the beginning. Sometimes it takes time and opportunity for two people to express how they really feel about each other, but no one is surprised when it finally happens.

Lines have to be blurred for real friends to become sexually intimate, and what was supposed to have been a real friendship was something else. If two people are real friends, there's no going back to what they had previously once they cross that line. What they knew about each other changed, and they'll never see each other the same way again. If one or the other gets involved with someone who comes into their social group, the atmosphere will be awkward when everyone is together, and the social dynamics will be strange.

Friends with benefits is acceptable in the hookup culture. Two people using each other to gratify an urge creates a "user-loser" relationship. It takes a certain type of personality to use someone for sex and think nothing's wrong with it. Friends giving sexual benefits to friends would be unacceptable anywhere but in a hookup culture. Would you really consider someone a friend whom you're having occasional sex with?

Women in the hookup culture who have occasional sex with particular men call them friends. But it's curious how the men are more realistic about the relationship and call it something different. Also, men and women in that culture don't establish friendships with the opposite sex unless they're physically unattractive to them, or a relative.

Growing and getting old in the culture

Men and women who grow up in the hookup culture and remain in that lifestyle establish a mentality that becomes a stronghold in their mind and life. Years pass quickly, and they mature into dirty old men lusting after young women, and cougars chasing men young enough to be their sons.

They never exercised restraint when they were young, and now they're old and are driven by the lusts of their youth. Pornography, which keeps your imagination engaged, and masturbation, which uses the imagination to keep the flesh alive, are tools of the enemy. Whatever you exercise gets stronger, and what you neglect gets weaker; therefore, it's important to understand that your mind is your strongest sexual organ.

Indulging your imagination with sexual images and fantasies will create strongholds in your mind that will remain active long after the body is unable to perform sexually. You'll end up in bondage to unfulfilled sexual urges that will be hard to bring under control.

All sexual acts outside of marriage are categorized as fornication. Sexual vice, sensual appetites, and unholy desires need to be harnessed, because they provoke those animal impulses that lead to out-of-control passions.

Abandon the vibrators and other sex toys. Throw out pornographic DVDs and magazines because those things keep you in bondage to sexual sins.

There's a price for ignoring God's standard for relationships, and casual sex, one-night stands and no commitments aren't what you were created for. Don't forsake your moral values by giving someone access to your body who isn't your husband or wife.

Remember that having multiple sexual partners doesn't work toward lasting relationships, but weakens the connections that should strengthen a union. Learn to guard the bonds that connect you to the person who may be right for you, and live without regret.

CHAPTER 4

I'll Know What I'm Looking for When I Find It

*Hope that is delayed makes you sad, but a wish
that comes true fills you with joy.*
—Proverbs 13:12 ERV

Relationship roulette

When someone says, "I'll know what I'm looking for when I find it," I think to myself, "Good luck finding what you don't know what you're looking for." There are so many personality types and traps to avoid, that if you don't know what you're looking for, you'll end up in a toxic game of relationship roulette.

Russian roulette is a game where you load a bullet into the chamber of a gun, spin the cylinder, point the gun at your head, and pull the trigger! If you don't kill yourself, you stay in the game until every player is eliminated and the last man is left standing.

Relationship roulette works by the same principle, but the exception is, the bullet in the chamber is one unhealthy relationship after another, that may not kill you, but will lead to PTRS, post-traumatic relationship stress.

Marriage and family therapist, Dr. Tarra Bates-Duford, said that PTRS happens at the end of a relationship when a person accepts that it's over. They feel alone, depressed, and uncertain about the future, and leave the relationship with heavy baggage.

Conflicting feelings for the former lover are what brings on the post-traumatic relationship stress. Duford goes on to say that it's natural to have regrets at the end of a relationship. I would add that even though there's emotional suffering, a soul tie developed. If they don't get free, they'll create collateral damage in their next relationship.

Collateral damage

Collateral damage is a term used for casualties inflicted on unintended targets. Two people beginning a new relationship are connecting with each other's past, present, and future. If there are unresolved issues from a past relationship, that baggage is brought into the new relationship.

Have you ever experienced an overreaction by someone you're involved with to something you said or did? You may have touched an emotional wound inflicted from a past relationship that hasn't healed yet. Their reaction may not be toward you, but to the person who wounded them. You've become the recipient of what someone else did, and a victim of collateral damage.

Child victims

Children become victims of collateral damage when divorced or single parents harbor bitterness after wrong partner choices. The children are emotionally victimized when they hear continual accusations about the other parent's faults.

Hearing and seeing those things can cause those children to grow up living out their parents' experience in their own relationships. The impression left on the child's mind creates an idea of how they should deal with their own situations, and they'll act and sound just like their parents.

They'll have trust issues and won't understand what a good relationship is supposed to be like, because they didn't grow up in a healthy environment. There are always exceptions to the rule, but the next story isn't one of them.

Two ships passing in the night

Have you heard the saying, "Two ships passing in the night?" Two ships passing in the night speaks of two people who meet for a brief but intense encounter, and never see each other again. It's two ships that greet each other while at sea, and sail off into the night.

There are no statistics that state the number of young men and women who leave home for an evening, and months later find out they're going to be parents. That ship found its way back into their harbor.

Every choice we make carries a consequence, and a moment of passion can bring some consequences that won't go away. When you don't consider the effects of your choices, they can tether you to someone for the rest of your life.

The young man and woman met earlier that evening, and by the end of the night, they were in bed together as consenting adults. When the DNA results came back 99.9 percent conclusive, he accepted it and took on his obligation as father to the child.

He wasn't interested in being in a relationship with someone he didn't really know, so the baby's mother did everything she could to make it difficult for him. When she wouldn't allow him to see his daughter, he took her to court, and the judge ordered visitation rights in his behalf. When the mother went into a rage, she was escorted out of the courtroom where she confronted him in the hallway screaming, "You're a dog, just like this one's father," speaking about the father of the child at her side. She then turned to his daughter, who was standing on the opposite side and said, "Your father is nothing but another sperm donor!" The children became victims of collateral damage.

The test-drive

I was speaking to a young woman about relationships and how to find the right person when she said, "You have to test-drive it before you buy it." Even though she thought what she said was clever, it was wrong on so many levels.

The thinking behind the test-drive is that you make sure you're sexually compatible with someone before you get into a committed relationship with them. How many people do you know who told you someone was a good lover, but for whatever reason, they aren't together today.

You can't build a relationship on good sex, even though people will argue that sex is an important part of a relationship, and I would agree. Sexual compatibility is important, but let's put things in their proper perspective. If you're physically attracted to someone, and the two of you communicate on a real level and understand each other, if you enjoy being with that person and share the same interests in the people, places, and things you like, you'll want to be in a committed relationship.

When two people connect mentally and emotionally, they'll most likely connect physically. That couple doesn't have to worry about sexual compatibility, because they connect in all the right places. But marriage should always be in the equation before you're sexually active.

Considering a test-drive, people aren't cars; but metaphorically, how many test-drives does it take before you're a used car? Any woman making decisions based on sexual performance doesn't understand her value as a person.

Men like to talk about their sexual exploits, and once word gets around that a young woman takes men on test-drives, she'll get popular for all the wrong reasons. In the end, no one wants a female with a bunch of miles on them.

Caveat emptor

Caveat emptor is Latin for "Let the buyer beware" or "Sold as is." A car salesman knows the best-looking cars on the lot sell faster; therefore, his motivation will be about presentation, because he wants to attract the eye of potential buyers.

Each used car needs a tune-up and paint job to make it appear more presentable. Did you know that plastic surgery, Botox, implants, and nip and tucks are like tune-ups and paint jobs? There's a reason why they call mascara makeup.

Mileage is also a factor in determining a car's value. Cars with higher mileage are considered less valuable than cars with lower mileage; therefore, a dishonest car salesman will turn back the odometer on a car to conceal the car's mileage, because every mile contributes to the wear and tear on that car. By mileage, you can estimate the life of a car, and under normal circumstances, even a used car with a few miles can be considered almost new. When physical attraction and sexual compatibility become the determining factors in choosing a partner, you as a buyer assume the risk that your relationship may not meet all of its overall expectation in total performance.

Making choices solely on appearance and sex, is like not asking for a car fax, or inquiring about the mileage. You won't have any information on how many accidents the car has been in, and you'll be dealing with someone who looks good on the outside, but needs repairs on the inside. "Caveat emptor," let the buyer beware!

Praying for the right person

Have you been praying that God would send you the right person? Praying for the right person is a good thing, but would you be ready if the right person came into your life in this season? God is about permanence, not temporary, so if all you want is a girl or boyfriend, wait until you're ready for something lasting.

Imagine if God moved according to your timing and not before He took the time to work things out for you while He worked His will into you. If you ended up in bed with the person you believed God sent you, would that tell you that neither one of you were ready?

Genesis said that the man and his wife were naked and weren't ashamed or embarrassed. They weren't ashamed or embarrassed, because they were married. Two people who end up in bed, who profess Jesus Christ as Lord and Savior, get embarrassed and ashamed when it's exposed.

God's desire is for you to be in the right relationship, and He'll prepare you before He gives you what you ask for. None of us are flawless, and there are always areas that need work, and God will never set you up for failure. In the meantime, remember that there are personality types and various traps to fall into if you don't know what you're looking for.

CHAPTER 5

Do Opposites Attract?

There are three things that are hard for me to understand—
really, four things that I don't understand: an eagle flying
in the sky, a snake moving on a rock, a ship moving across
the ocean, and a man in love with a woman.
—Proverbs 30:18–19 ERV

An eagle flying in the sky, a snake moving on a rock, a ship moving across the ocean, and a man in love with a woman, are four things that have no traceable paths, unless you know their origin and their destination.

In the same way, it's hard to figure out how two people who obviously aren't compatible got together, unless you know how they began, or believe that opposites attract.

The idea that opposites attract was introduced in the 1950s as an argument by a psychologist named Robert Francis Winch. The psychologist did a study on married couples and concluded that it wasn't similarities that made their relationship work, but their differences that kept them together. But that isn't an accurate assessment.

Men and women are attracted to people with qualities and interests similar to their own. So what would bring two people who are different together? The answer is attraction, but not in the way that Winch thought.

Eye candy

The first known use of the term *eye candy* was in 1978, and was used as a description for two physically attractive women on a television show called *Three's Company*.

These two young women were very intelligent, but entertained their audience by playing pretty girls that weren't too smart. The writers wanted to appeal to the eyes more than the mind; therefore, the term *eye candy* was used to describe the roles of the two young women.

At some point, every man and woman will have to get beyond what pleases their eyes, to what's most important, who a person is. But even then, our initial impression of someone will influence how we view them.

It's good to get another person's opinion when assessing someone, and get some background information before getting involved with them. But if you can't get beyond a physical attraction, your first impressions can cause you to assign characteristics to that person according to how you see them.

I had an amusing experience with a friend. He was injured and couldn't work, and while convalescing at home, he got hooked on the daytime soaps. A person named Susan Lucci played the character Erica Kane on one of these soap operas. On this particular day, he seemed distracted and irritated. When I asked him what the matter was, he told me that he hated Erica Kane, and what he would do if he ever saw her!

I laughed every time I thought about it, because he forgot that she's an actor, and couldn't separate the character from the real person. Applying that to people we meet, we need to give ourselves enough time to separate the "act" from the real person. We can be like that with first impressions.

It's hard to get beyond our negative impression of someone if that's how we view them in the beginning. Likewise, a positive impression of someone can cause us to overlook their negatives, and that's one of the ways opposites attract. Even if bad behavior persists, it may be too late if you're already invested in that person.

Compatibly incompatible

Another way opposites attract, is when two people have the right mental and emotional makeup to be in a dysfunctional relationship. I call that being compatibly incompatible, which may sound like an oxymoron, but those types of people can be together even though their personalities are in constant conflict.

Those types of people have the right mindset to continue in a relationship that someone of a different mindset would never tolerate. But again, people with the right mental and emotional makeup will hang in there when someone else would walk away.

You may know a couple who fits that description, and if you do, you know that they always find a good reason to continue together. It happens more than you think, and again, how they process what's going on makes them compatible even though they're incompatible.

Reason and logic don't help in that type of relationship, because they don't think like you, or they wouldn't be together. Your prayers don't work in that situation, because you're praying against that couple's will. It would be better for you to pray for your own patience and long-suffering, so that you can wait for them to come to an end, instead of injecting yourself into their dysfunction.

CHAPTER 6

Personality Types You May Recognize

How much better to get wisdom than gold,
to get insight rather than silver!
—Proverbs 16:16 NIV

There will be certain personality types you'll encounter when meeting and interacting with people socially and personally. You need to be aware of what you're dealing with, in order to avoid a relationship with someone that may be very toxic.

This chapter doesn't cover every personality type you may encounter, but it will give you valuable information about the most common personality types you'll come in contact with. Remember, "whatever you allow, you have to live with."

The player

Words can be used to emotionally manipulate you, and people who know how to use words are called players. The two most famous players are Casanova and Don Juan.

Casanova went after women who were accessible and easy, enjoying intense moments of pleasure with them. But Don Juan went for virgins, nuns, women who were hard to get, and women who belonged to other men.

These two men practiced the art of romance and knew that gullible and naive females believed what they wanted to hear. Therefore, I'll remind the reader that Proverbs chapter 4, verse 23 (NIV) says, "Above all else, guard your heart, for everything you do flows from it."

When dealing with players, there could be more going on than what's on the surface. There can be underlying issues that are causing that type of behavior. Relationships are built around a person's desires, but why would anyone want to play with someone's heart?

Playing heart games is a sign of someone having flawed thoughts and feelings that lead to those types of action. Consider compulsive sexual behavior or sexual addiction. That person is focused on their own sexual fantasies and need more than one partner to fulfill them. You're important in the total scheme of things, so it's not as if they don't want you, because they do, but you're not enough. A female who practiced this behavior would be called a nymphomaniac.

There's another type of player who gains personal satisfaction by knowing they can control someone emotionally. Those are the types who when they're finished with you, you get thrown away. Does that sound like someone who can be easily analyzed?

The liar

A rose is still a rose by any other name; and a lie is still a lie, whether it's a big lie, a little lie, or a white lie. You can call it a fib, a falsehood, or an untruth; but a lie still misleads, gives false accounts, and conceals the truth.

Lies bring you in circles and lead you away from truth, and if you were more confused after a conversation with someone than before you began, you were probably hearing a lie.

Someone telling the truth wants you to understand, and will try to be as clear as possible. But liars are continually covering, diverting, and focusing on something other than the issue.

Lies are evidence of a transgression because they're used to protect the violator from exposure. Therefore, lying becomes essential to the liar as a defense. But telling a single lie doesn't make one a pathological or habitual liar. A single instance of lying merely indicates that a person lied at that moment. Pathological liars, on the other hand, are people who have made lying a habit and a way of life.

Did you know that a lie deceives the person telling the lie? The liar has to convince themselves of the lie first, and once they're convinced, they'll use it on you.

Anyone in a relationship with a liar, and finds out what that person is, should end the relationship immediately. But again, you have to live with whatever you allow.

A person in a relationship with a liar should know that the end of a lie brings shame, embarrassment, and finally, exposure. Lies always expose the person telling the lie, and you'll have to deal with who that person really is.

In the end, truth always sets you free from a lie, though you may get hurt before that happens.

The riddler

Who gives you hints, with answers concealed? Understand this riddle, and the truth is revealed. Who states a fact, without saying it's true? Figure that out and who's talking to you.

Starting a new relationship gives you an opportunity to meet your love interest's circle of friends. If and when that happens, keep your eyes open for the person who may engage you in a strange conversation after you become their friend, because new relationships aren't always as they appear in the beginning.

You can be in the dark about certain things, and the riddler is a warning sign concerning those things. It may sound strange, but riddlers have moral boundaries that prevent them from standing by and watching while you're kept in the dark about something that isn't right. They may never come right out and say what it is, because they were friends with your love interest before they met you. Instead, they'll drop hints and make suggestions about things you should look out for.

In their own way, riddlers address issues that they don't agree with, and in the end, you'll understand what they were trying to warn you about.

Riddlers can be the type of people you may not want to have anything to do with because they knew what was going on and didn't tell you. But riddlers can also give you that needed warning sign if you're paying attention.

Dr. Frankenstein

Dr. Frankenstein is a fictional horror story about a gifted scientist who was insane. He was obsessed with creating his own man, and would sneak into graveyards at night and steal body parts from dead corpses.) Eventually, he was successful with his experiment, but what he created wasn't what he imagined it to be.

There are people like Dr. Frankenstein who aren't fictional or insane, but they try to create their new love interest into something they want them to be. They'll go to the graveyards of old relationships and dig up a former lover in an attempt to fit parts of their character onto their new love interest.

The Frankenstein personality type isn't gender-specific, because there are also women who try to recreate men into what they want them to look, talk, and act like. You might say, "Maybe there are some things about him she needed to change," but these changes are all about what the Frankenstein personality type wants, and not who that person is.

You would think it should be easier to find what they're looking for instead of making someone over, but that doesn't work with this personality type, because they want their own creation. They'll change how you look, correct the way you talk, and even criticize your style of dress if it doesn't agree with them. But knowing who you are, keeps you from becoming what someone else wants you to be, and not knowing who you are, can cause you to become something for someone else.

Everyone is unique, and even though two people can be alike, we're still individually different. That's what makes you who you are, and should keep you from becoming what someone else wants you to be.

Dr. Jekyll and Mr. Hyde

Dr. Jekyll and Mr. Hyde is a story about the duplicity of human nature. Dr. Jekyll, like Dr. Frankenstein, was also a scientist who meddled in the dark side of science.

Dr. Jekyll experimented with freeing the suppressed alter ego in men by ingesting a potion he created, and Mr. Hyde, who was his alter ego, would emerge.

The Hyde personality acted on his lower impulses and was physically aggressive toward everyone, especially women. A woman who felt safe in the presence of Dr. Jekyll was shocked when Hyde emerged. There are men who are predators, who conduct themselves in a socially acceptable way in public, but in a private situation, they'll change when alone with the opposite sex.

Statistics show that one out of six women will most likely be a victim of an attempted or a completed sexual assault. That statistic doesn't factor in women of other countries.

Women should always let someone know where they're going and who they're with when out on a first date. They should have their own money, cell phone, and a way home if things go wrong. It should also be a rule that young women let the other person know up front, that their date is for enjoyment, and not for sex.

Take time to get to know the person you're going out with, because who a person is in public, may not be who they are in private.

The romantic

Imagine fireworks on New Year's Eve, with all the thrills and spills of a roller coaster ride before pulling into the station. That's the adrenaline rush romantics have with each new love interest. The length of time they're on that endorphin high determines how in love they are in that moment. Afterward comes the business of settling into a relationship.

A romantic person always chases the magic of the moment, because they're in love with being in love. Like Eros and Cupid, romantics are searching for that mythical love written about in romance novels and movies.

Romantics are usually females who spend a lot of time reading love novels and imagining the perfect scenario for a romantic encounter. Anyone in a relationship with this personality type needs to remember to write love notes and send flowers. Public displays of affection, PDAs, with bunches of hugs and kisses are surely welcome and expected; but if you're a private person, a romantic person may not be for you, because they need someone who's willing to show their affection openly.

Don't be surprised if you can't keep up with the level of passionate energy they long for, because romantics are adrenaline junkies and will accuse you of being distant and cold if you don't reciprocate.

When she says that the relationship isn't working, and you find her snuggled in the arms of someone new, remember that it wasn't that she wasn't serious, but that she found herself in an unexpected romantic encounter that she needed to explore.

The needy person

Needy people bring a lot of emotional baggage into a relationship, because they are insecure, need constant affirmation, and crave unwavering attention. It's common for a needy person to continually call and text, and when you don't respond fast enough, it's interpreted as rejection.

A needy person will always be emotionally ahead of you. While you're considering the relationship, they're invested. When you're in talk, they're in touch; and when you're in like, they're in love. A simple conversation can turn into something more than expected if you're not careful. Friendliness can be interpreted as sexual attraction, and before you know it, you may hear rumors that the two of you are getting together.

People who like someone running after them and being the center of attention will enjoy this personality type. But normally, most people would feel suffocated, because a relationship with a needy person can be mentally and emotionally exhausting.

Suggestions of scaling it back doesn't work because that can throw a needy person into crisis mode, and anyone trying to leave that type of relationship will find it difficult if they don't like emotional scenes.

When someone makes you feel guilty for their emotional state, it's called emotional blackmail. The needy person will resort to emotional blackmail to manipulate their partner, by suggesting that something may happen to them if the partner leaves.

Some of them have gone so far as to make an attempt at hurting themselves. If something like that happens, you're dealing with a mentally unstable person, and you should stay away from them, because you're not responsible for another person's actions, and it's also their way of controlling the relationship.

Waiting for the right time to get free from this personality type may never come, because they'll do anything to keep you. But if you're a "user," you're a perfect match for a needy person.

The user

Physical attraction, communication, or social compatibility are not issues for a user personality type. Your resources are what attracts them, and how they can use them determines your compatibility. It's all about need and supply.

Users can be both male and female, but they call female users gold diggers on the higher end, and "handouts" on the lower.

Sometimes a relationship that isn't working can become a user relationship when two people realize they aren't compatible, but stay together out of convenience. Both people are using each other to some degree, and anyone in a relationship because it's fulfilling some financial or material need is a user.

Friends and family of someone in a user relationship have no success with their interventions. They become frustrated when their friend or family member ignores that they're being used. Telling the person they're being used, is met with accusations of "You don't want me to have anybody," because as long as they give the user what they want, the user will stay.

Users are usually disliked by the friends and family of the person being used, but they don't feel guilty about it. You're dealing with a different kind of person, and they understand that showing a certain amount of affection and romance are a part of their obligation. They're willing to prostitute themselves to make sure the person they're using is satisfied. Again, a user and a needy person are a perfect match.

The jealous person

When you're dealing with a jealous person, you're dealing with fear, insecurity, suspicion, and pride. Be careful to answer texts and your cell if they call you, because those things can turn into something serious. Also, be where you say you're going to be, just in case they decide to check in on you.

A jealous person will feel disrespected, and think you believe they're a fool if you show too much interest in a friend of the opposite sex in their presence. A jealous female may purposely have an affair to get even for a perceived encounter, that was no more than a friendly exchange. Jealousy can even result in violence, if the jealous person's anger gets out of control. That makes it important to know what lines not to cross when you're in a relationship with a jealous person.

We all will have feelings of jealousy when a valuable relationship is threatened by a third party, but whether real or imagined, what puts someone in the category of being a jealous person, is that jealousy has become their distinguishing quality of character.

A jealous person and a flirt form a toxic relationship. An innocent man can be drawn in by the flirtatious partner, and find himself in a physical conflict with her man. People who find themselves in a relationship with a jealous person will become aware of it early in the relationship. That's when it's time to decide whether to adjust how you interact with others socially, or leave the relationship altogether.

The retaliator

Retaliators aren't looking for resolve; they want revenge! They believe the best remedy for a problem is to give you a taste of your own medicine. If you cheat on them, they'll cheat on you. If you don't make time for them, they won't make time for you. Whatever you do to them, they'll do to you, which is never the way to work through issues. But for the retaliator it's reactionary, because they've already determined how they'll act in certain situations.

Retaliators have suspicious natures, are contentious, and always on guard. They're most likely child witnesses of their parents' bad choices who suffer from collateral damage, and have grown up to live out their parents' experiences in their own relationships.

Their suspicious nature prevents them from forming healthy relationships even if a partner proves to be faithful, because they have a wait-and-see attitude. It takes time and patience to get a retaliator to trust you, because of fear of being taken advantage of. Therefore, a retaliator can end up sabotaging their own relationship from the beginning.

The retaliator personality type is usually female, but men of the same character have a more direct and aggressive response to a perceived slight. A female retaliator may destroy something of yours in an act of revenge, but not every retaliator reacts in the same way. However, it is a retaliator trait to respond in kind when violated.

The compromiser

In every relationship, there's going to be a time of compromise to settle a situation. But the compromiser personality type is never given equal consideration in a disagreement because their partner knows they would rather give in and avoid a conflict.

This creates problems for the friends and family of the compromiser, because they know that their loved one will get taken advantage of if they're with the wrong person. The compromiser personality type isn't weak; they just think it's better to give in to keep peace, because they don't like to argue. The compromiser isn't who we're concerned with as much as the selfish person, they may get involved with.

If there's no resolve and nothing changes, it's not a healthy relationship. Healthy relationships affirm what both people hold as important, to satisfy each other's mutual needs. Unhealthy relationships demand that one partner change to accommodate the other, by ignoring, or suppressing how their partner feels.

Someone who doesn't allow you to be yourself isn't correctly matched for you, and a negative personality type will take advantage of a compromiser.

The codependent

A person who's a supporter, rescuer, and a keeper of secrets to protect another person is most likely in a codependent relationship. The codependent person needs the dependent person to rely on them, which gives the codependent a sense of purpose.

A codependent needs to feel needed, and resists any attempts to change their interactions with the dependent person. Their support of the actions of the dependent person stands in the way of positive change, and they become enablers.

The term codependent isn't a positive label; it's obstructive, and family and friends on both sides of the individuals involved get drawn into their toxic relationship when they don't understand the dynamics of this union. Nothing good comes out of this type of relationship.

The dependent partner's dysfunction takes priority over everything in the codependent's life, and they'll provide things that uphold the dependent person's negative lifestyle. Once the codependent person is removed from the equation, it won't be long before the dependent partner will feel the consequences of their bad decisions. Hopefully, they'll seek change.

The reality is that the codependent person needs someone to depend on them, as much as the dependent person needs the codependent. If you want to see change, you'll have to organize an intervention and get the codependent to stop what they're doing.

These types of relationships are unhealthy, and will drive friends and family apart. It never ends well, and if you know someone who is codependent in someone's dysfunction, you may have to separate yourself from that situation for your own mental health.

Jonah

The Jonah personality type will create obstacles in the lives of purpose driven people. Storms and turmoil follow Jonah because he's out of the will of God, and won't do what he should, in order to prevent those storms from following him. If you're a goal-driven person, don't allow a Jonah on your boat!

If you ever hear of someone that had a bright future, but allowed a trouble ridden person in their life, it's probably because they let Jonah on their boat. This personality type doesn't necessarily have to be a male; a Jonah can be female. Jonah doesn't intentionally sabotage your plans, but the storms that follow them get you caught in their turbulence.

Purpose-driven people can lose sight of their goals when they get involved with a Jonah, and the number of problems they're having can be traced back to the moment Jonah came into their life. You may want to help, but you'll find yourself working harder than them, because they'll find time to sleep in the midst of the storm.

It may sound harsh, but Jonah needs to be thrown overboard before he or she sinks your ship. Let God deal with Jonah.

The narcissist

The narcissistic personality type gets its name from a story in Greek mythology. Narcissists have so many layers to their personality, that anyone who finds themselves in a relationship with a narcissist will be confused about what they're dealing with.

According to Greek mythology, Narcissus was a hunter and the son of the river god Cephissus and Liriope, the nymph.

One day as Narcissus hunted in the woods, the nymph Echo saw him and immediately fell in love with him. When Echo attempted to embrace and kiss him, Narcissus rejected her and pushed her away. In hopeless anguish, Echo roamed through the woods until her life faded away, leaving nothing but the sound of an echo.

Nemesis, the goddess of retribution and revenge, heard what happened to Echo, and sought to punish Narcissus for his lack of empathy by showing him a pool of water that reflected his own image back to him. Narcissus fell in love with his image, but realized that he could never find someone as satisfying as himself, and out of despair, committed suicide.

Narcissists lack the ability to understand or empathize with the feelings of anyone but themselves. A narcissistic person will never admit to being wrong, and if there's a problem in the relationship, it's because of you. They refuse to acknowledge any shortcomings in character or act.

Narcissists live in a world where everything revolves around them, and as far as they're concerned, you'll never meet anyone like them; so you should feel privileged that they chose you as their partner. They need to feel as important to you as they do to themselves, and if you don't treat them that way, they have no need of you.

Narcissists crave admiration and praise, and if you're in a relationship with one, don't expect them to reciprocate unless it makes them look good, and never embarrass them. Don't expect your narcissistic partner to be there for you if it doesn't benefit them. It's also important to understand that narcissists create their own realities, and what they say is true, and not what you think or see. Are you familiar with the term *gaslighting*?

There's a biblical example of perfect narcissism. The angel Lucifer which means "Shining One" or "Light Bearer," was transformed into a creature of darkness called Satan and the devil, because he was exalted in his own beauty, and lead a rebellion against God.

Ezekiel 28:14–17 (NKJV) says,

> You *were* the anointed cherub who covers,
> I established you;
> You were on the holy mountain of God;
> You walked back and forth in the midst of fiery
> stones.
> You *were* perfect in your ways from the day you
> were created,
> Till iniquity was found in you.
>
> By the abundance of your trading
> You became filled with violence within,
> And you sinned;
> Therefore I cast you as a profane thing
> Out of the mountain of God;
> And I destroyed you, O covering cherub,
> From the midst of the fiery stones.
>
> Your heart was lifted up because of your beauty;
> You corrupted your wisdom for the sake of your
> splendor;
> I cast you to the ground,

I laid you before kings,
That they might gaze at you.

In those verses, we get a glimpse into the complex nature of a narcissistic spirit. Lucifer's beauty was only a part of a much darker issue. The scriptures tell us that Lucifer was perfect in his ways from the day he was created, till iniquity was found in him.

Iniquity is a bending or twisting away from God's standard of righteousness. So we see that there was more going on than the issue of beauty. There were things happening in Lucifer that twisted his perception of himself into something other than what God created him to be.

When dealing with a narcissistic personality type, you're dealing with someone who has more going on inside than what is evident. I believe that you'll find many people with some narcissistic traits, but Lucifer is the archetype. Anyone who's been in a relationship with a narcissist would find it hard to put their finger on one thing that would describe this complex personality type. My advice would be to run away, hide, and avoid any contact with them.

The abuser

Abusers can either be male or female, but the most common abusers are male. Abuse is not only physical, but it can also be emotional or psychological. It's important that we put abuse in its proper context according to this book, in order to deal with this subject correctly.

In order for something to rise to the level of abuse, there has to be an earnest intention to engage in psychological or emotional manipulation, deliberate cruelty, or habitual violence. It's also important to remember that impulsive anger can cause you to act out of character and be disrespectful to your partner, which can be considered abusive.

The true nature of an abuser is to misuse someone because of something in their background that shaped the way they interact with their partner, or a psychological disorder that causes an emotional reaction that they believe controls a situation. No matter what the reason, there are deeper things at play.

An abuser may appear self-confident and express strong opinions and beliefs in their discourses with others, but someone with strong opinions isn't necessarily an abuser; some men are simply confident assertive people that women may find attractive.

A warning sign would be seeing that confident male respond negatively to an assertive woman with a different opinion than theirs. Abusers feel that women are beneath their consideration, and it's a sign of disrespect to be challenged by a woman.

Female abusers have a disdain for confident men, and welcome any opportunity to embarrass them in public. For her, it's intolerable to listen to them talk for too long, and she'll intentionally attempt to offend them. In our society, it's acceptable for a female to humiliate a man in public, but unacceptable for a man to do the same to a woman. This gives her an advantage that she'll exercise to the fullest. But whether the abuser is male or female, abusers reveal themselves by how they act with the opposite sex.

An abusive relationship doesn't necessarily start out abusive, but slowly escalates over time. The relationship may appear normal in the beginning, but as time passes, there will be a noted difference in the way both people conduct themselves in public.

The body language of the abused persons will appear withdrawn in the presence of their abusers, and they'll seem overly cautious about what they say and do. This can be interpreted as being quiet and shy if you don't know that person, but people who do, know that's not how they normally act, and something is wrong.

Once the relationship escalates to that point, the abuser will attempt to cut off access from friends and family, and will monitor all the contacts of their partner. Abusers will often indulge in abusive sex and ignore their partner's discomfort. The abuser enjoys controlling their partner physically while having sex, and use demeaning language to degrade them.

The female abuser will withhold sex as a punishment, and consent as a reward. But even in rewarding her partner, she'll emotionally disengage to demonstrate power over him.

Male and female abuser micromanage their partner's spending habits. If the partner is financially independent, that's a form of empowerment that needs to be brought under control by the abuser. It's not that they want their money, because abusers view any dependence on their partner as a weakness. It's about control!

A person who allows themselves to remain in an abusive relationship frustrates the efforts of their friends' and family's interventions. But there's a difference between a person with a victim mentality and someone who refuses to be a victim. The victim becomes afraid and submits to their abuser, but the person who refuses to be a victim gets angry and won't tolerate it.

The Jezebel spirit

In interpersonal relationships, the Jezebel spirit would most likely be a woman; but in areas of service, it could be a man. Ahab, who was king of Israel, married Jezebel, the daughter of the king of Tyre. Ahab was king, but Jezebel was the power behind his throne.

There are those who would liken this personality type to a witch, and traditionally, you envision a witch dressed in black wearing a high pointed black hat with a long ugly nose on her face, with a mole on the end of it. But Jezebel doesn't do incantations or cast spells; her power is exercising control over everyone in her sphere of influence through psychological manipulation and intimidation.

The desire for power and control over events and people is the root of witchcraft, and Jezebels need an Ahab to have that power. This personality type looks for men in positions of authority whose power they can use for their benefit.

The Jezebel personality type doesn't want a man she can't influence, and if the man she's with isn't influential, he'll be her floor mat. She'll also make partner choice decisions for her friends and children if she has any.

Men with women that were friends of the Jezebel personality, can attest to the influence she held over their women, and how hard it was to break that influence. If you're her friend, and she doesn't approve of your partner, she'll either treat him with contempt, or go as far as attempting to seduce him to prove you made a wrong choice. Some may call this person a control freak, but this personality type goes much deeper than that.

The carnal Christian

Did you know that everyone who goes to church doesn't go for the same reasons? There are men who go to church to get a Christian woman. Likewise, some women go to church to meet men who are Christian. But where you meet someone doesn't necessarily translate into having the same religious beliefs and morals.

There are people with different levels of spiritual maturity in the church, and if that's where you're going fishing, you can end up with a fish that you're going to have to scale.

Judas was a disciple, and Mary Magdalene had seven devils before Jesus cast them out. Phinehas and Hophni were preacher's sons who were having sex with the women in the congregation. So, we hear about all the hypocrites in the church, but where did they come from?

The Church is a place where believers assemble and people seeking salvation come to get saved. Therefore, you have a congregation that may have been hypocrites before they came, and brought their hypocrisy with them. I'm convinced that you'll find more hypocrites outside of the church, than on the inside.

It's important to remember that the people inside the church are in the process of transformation, and until that happens, the church gets a bad reputation.

Take for instance social media posts and pictures of young Christian men and women at the clubs and other places, drinking, dancing, and partying. But they profess Jesus Christ as their Lord and Savior. To an onlooking and judgmental world, these people aren't a good testimony for Christ, because the unsaved will judge the entire Church by them.

Even though these Christians have accepted Jesus as their savior, he hasn't become their lord, and nothing changes in their life except their Christian profession, and attending church on Sundays. These are the types of Christians that can take a sincere child of God off course as fast and effectively, as an unbeliever.

Club Broadway

To go to Club Broadway, you have to take the first left off Straight Street, which makes it easy to see the neon sign from Narrow Way Drive. The club is located on Broadway Boulevard, in Babylon County.

Club Broadway is a place where sinners and carnal Christians can mingle and enjoy themselves. Greeters are waiting at the door to take your entrance offering, and the ministers attending the bar serve communion.

There's a wide and spacious dance floor for praise and worship, and worship leader DJ will play the best praise music beats. All your friends who are living in darkness and other carnal Christian will be there, so you don't have to worry about being judged, because like spirits attract; and if you're not like them, they won't like you.

If you were to ask them, "Why do you go there?" They'll tell you not to judge them because God knows their heart." But I guess they never read Isaiah 29:13, which says,

The Lord says:

"These people come near to me with their mouth
and honor me with their lips,
but their hearts are far from me.
Their worship of me
is based on merely human rules they have been
taught." (NIV)

CHAPTER 7

The Five Steps

*Let the wise hear and increase in learning, and the
one who understands obtain guidance.*
—Proverbs 1:5 ESV

The expression "Love is blind," speaks to the idea that people in love can't see the faults of the person they're in love with, and that's true in many cases. But there's a social experiment that puts a different twist on that idea.

This experiment challenges their participants to make a connection with someone without seeing who they're talking to. Single men and women come together in pods and communicate by sharing things about themselves. They're allowed to ask each other personal questions and talk with multiple people until the playing field is narrowed down to one person.

Once they've decided which person is for them, they can request that person's hand in marriage. If the answer is yes, they can see who they were talking to. But one of the biggest fears is, will this person be attractive to me, and will I be attractive to them?

Some of the men and women participating in the experiment, know they made a mistake the moment they see the person they chose, because that person didn't look anything like they envisioned them to look. Others feel they made the wrong choice once they're away on their paid honeymoon vacation, which is the next step in the process, and find out that the person is different from who they were in the pods.

After the honeymoon vacation, each couple is required to live together until the actual marriage ceremony.

Leaving that controlled environment to live together, is where everything that was said in the pods gets tested by reality. Also, by meeting and talking with each other's friends and family before the wedding day is a part of the process, and gives each couple a different look at the person they chose.

Up until that point, the relationship was based on what was said in the pods; therefore, returning to reality proves if what they experienced in the pods was conceptual or real.

Five steps to a good relationship

There are five steps that everyone takes from the start, to establishing a relationship. The five steps are attraction, communication, socialization, commitment, and the last step is marriage.

Most of us aren't aware of what we're doing, and that's what gets us into trouble! Taking these steps in their proper order will help you navigate towards good partner choices. Likewise, when these five steps are taken out of order, it increases the chances of making a wrong choice. Also, moving through the steps impulsively without giving each step time to prove itself, will cause you to commit prematurely.

Step 1. Attraction is the first step in the five steps to a good relationship. "Do you like what you see?" How can you start a relationship with someone you aren't attracted to? Therefore, no matter what anyone says, looks do matter; and attraction is the beginning of your partner choice, but not where it ends.

Step 2. Communication is the second step. "Can you talk?" How can you build a relationship with someone you can't talk to? Communication is a relationship builder, and the thread that holds every step together going forward.

A conversation can either validate or cancel out what attracts you about a person; therefore, after seeing or meeting someone, you need to spend time talking to them.

Step 3. Socialization is the third step. "What do you have in common in the people, places, and things you like?" Communication will validate or cancel out your attraction for someone, but if you decide to continue, socialization connects what you see and hear with a practical experience.

Socialization gives you an opportunity to see a different side of a person by sharing time together through dating, and other social activities. It helps you determine if you enjoy each other's company.

Step 4. Commitment is the fourth step. "How serious are you willing to get?" Taking time to get to know one another helps you decide if you want to bring your relationship to another level, or keep things status quo. Your person may or may not have checked the first three boxes, so it's up to you to decide how you'll proceed.

A committed relationship is an investment in a future with someone, so it's important to consider wisely.

Step 5. Marriage is the fifth and final step in the five steps to a good relationship. The question "Will you marry me?" speaks to the value a person holds in your life, because marriage is a true desire for permanence.

Again, every relationship should have a destination, and marriage should be the destination and consummation of a committed relationship.

Transient relationships

Transient relationships are relationships that can end today, tomorrow, next month, or at any time. These types of relationships are temporary but can go on indefinitely. Until marriage becomes your destination, every relationship you have is considered transient, and most relationships we see today are transient.

Committing to anything other than marriage is like signing a long-term contract in a temporary situation. You've locked yourself down to the obligation of a marriage, without a ring, a wedding date, or any legal rights of support. You don't even need a divorce to walk away.

Two people can find themselves in transient relationships because of sexual involvement. Bad bonding causes young men and women to get sexually involved in step one and two, emotionally entangled by step three, and living together by step four. But each of these steps has their transition points, and if you aren't aware of them, you'll be among those who wonder how they got themselves into the type of relationship they're in.

Transition points

Every relationship has identifiable things that signal changes in your interactions with each other. I call these changes transition points.

A transition indicates something different is happening in your relationship, and not being aware of these changes will cause you to find yourself in something you may not have been ready for. When you're not aware that friendly exchanges are becoming more personal, and affectionate banter is more intimate, you're missing that your friendship is transitioning. Your friend may become territorial and seem jealous when people of the opposite sex get too close. Deeper feelings may be surfacing which isn't a bad thing if you're on the same page, but it's a problem if you're not.

Also, when someone is transitioning away, physical distancing happens, followed by unfamiliar responses to touch and other things that were familiar between the two of you. Distancing is a sign that the relationship may be ending.

Timing is also important in understanding changes in a relationship. Knowing when it's the right time for you, and making it clear to the other person, keeps you on the same page because you don't want to get ahead of each other.

It's in your power to control the momentum of your relationship by giving each step time to work itself through. Be sure to evaluate your relationship at each step, and don't make the mistake of taking the steps out of order.

Hopscotch

Are you familiar with a children's game called hopscotch? Children playing hopscotch take turns hopping in and over ten squares marked on the ground. There are single and double squares, and only one foot can be in a square at a time, unless your feet land in a double square.

A marker or bean bag is thrown into one of the squares, and the child has to hop on one leg over the square with the marker or bean bag in it and retrieve that marker or bean bag on the way back. The goal of the game is to hop to the end square and back on one leg without your other foot touching the ground.

There are men and women that hop in and out of relationships retrieving former lovers on the rebound like playing hopscotch. If a person doesn't know what they want, they'll have their feet in double squares, and even children playing hopscotch know the rules, and if you don't follow them, they won't play with you.

It's difficult to find the right person until you know what you want. Bad bonding, premature commitments, and emotional obligations, will have you tethered to someone you're still getting to know. Again, becoming sexually intimate with a person before you know them socially will cause you to be emotionally tied to a stranger in an ungodly soul tie.

Warning signs and red flags

A warning sign indicates that problems are ahead, and a red flag means danger because of an issue that requires immediate attention. But not everyone has the same standard for what they will, or will not allow, and what may be a deal-breaker for you, may not be a deal-breaker for someone else.

You'd be surprised at how many people don't give immediate attention to what is obviously a red flag, but instead, view it as a warning sign. People that are emotionally invested ignore warning signs, and allow red flags to go unresolved. They disregard stop signs, and blow through red lights and don't understand how they got injured.

Each individual has to determine what their limits are, because it's hard to walk away from a relationship after you're emotionally invested. Therefore, don't commit to a person that hasn't met your expectations.

Boundaries should be established for anyone that you're in a relationship with, and they should know how to treat you, and how you want the relationship to go. This gives each person the opportunity to decide if they want that too. Understanding what lines aren't to be crossed, shows a respect for boundaries, because clear communication ensures that no one is confused by mixed messaging. But I would be curious to know, would you be willing to walk away if your love interest crossed a line?

CHAPTER 8

Do You Like What You See?

*A woman may seem to be beautiful, but that can deceive
people. Her body will not be beautiful forever, but a woman
who respects the Lord with fear will receive honour.*
—Proverbs 31:30 EASY

As I said in chapter 7, "How can you start a relationship with someone you aren't attracted to?" After all, looks do matter.

What a person looks like is significant in forming a relationship, but it's also important that you understand the progressive stages of attraction before you make the mistake of thinking good looks make a person. A study published by Madeleine Fugere, a social psychologist, found that physical appearance greatly influenced decisions concerning dating, and men and women will go after people they consider more attractive than less attractive.

Our initial attraction centers around appearance, but attraction is more than what you see. Attraction also has a cognitive side to it, which is a mental process that acquires knowledge through considering, reasoning, and judging someone, and then afterwards, you form an impression.

When you meet an attractive person and get to know them, what holds your attention is their unique qualities of character. A pleasant personality and personal achievements can add to someone's attractiveness, and the person that didn't look so good in the beginning, may start to look better after you discover more about them.

It's important not to form an opinion of someone entirely on appearance, because you can attribute favorable qualities to people you consider attractive, rich, and famous, and unfavorable qualities to people whom you see as less attractive.

Projecting

We have a way of attributing our idea of what someone is like before we actually get to know them, which is called first impressions. What we're really doing, is imagining what we perceive that person to be, and projecting that onto them. That type of judgment will cause you to form an opinion of someone that's more than they deserve, or less than they're worthy of. Have you ever met a very attractive person, and after a conversation thought to yourself, "You looked better before you started talking!" It's important to get beyond the illusion of visual attraction and come to an understanding of who a person really is.

There was a song released called "Just My Imagination" by a group called The Temptations. This song reflects the fantasies that so many men and women create in their mind around someone they've seen, thought was beautiful, but never met.

The storyline was about a young man who saw a woman through his window, and fell in love with the idea of who he imagined her to be. In his mind, he created a life where they lived in the country and were happy ever after. Everything in this song was based on this imagination. Here are the lyrics to the song.

> Each day through my window, I watch her as she
>   passes by
> I say to myself, "You're such a lucky guy"
> To have a girl like her is truly a dream come true
> Out of all the fellows in the world, she belongs
>   to you

But it was just my imagination
Running away with me
It was just my imagination
Running away with me
Soon we'll be married, and raise a family
And have a cozy little home out in the country,
    with two children, maybe three
I tell you I can visualize it all
This couldn't be a dream, for too real it all seems

But it was just my imagination, once again
Running way with me
Tell you it was just my imagination
Running away with me

Every night on my knees I pray
Dear Lord, hear my plea
Don't ever let another take her love from me
Or I would surely die
Her love is heavenly, when her arms enfold me
I hear a tender rhapsody
But in reality, she doesn't even know me
Just my imagination once again
Running way with me
Tell you it was just my imagination
Running away with me

The young man's attraction for this young woman wasn't the problem. The problem was he projected all those things unto that young woman without any knowledge of who she really was.

Attraction may be the first step in starting a relationship, but you can't build a relationship on attraction alone. Attraction arouses an interest to know more about a person, but a conversation will either affirm, or disappoint your attraction.

Attraction is a process of discovery, and what may be attractive to you, may not be as appealing to someone else. What appeals to someone is subject to their own individual taste, and you may discover that you're attracted to certain personality types, or particular physical attributes. Not everyone knows when or how it began.

Certain skin tones or hair colors may attract you, and some men and women may be attracted to people of different cultures; but regardless of what attracts you, attraction is subjective, personal, and a process of discovery.

Most of us don't know how or when we began to prefer certain types, but left to itself and void of racial bias and prejudice, attraction transcends social norms, cultural influence, and language barriers.

Racial bias and prejudice based on a person's ethnicity or skin color are practices passed on by those who learned them. Those opinions can cause someone's personal preferences to be influenced and suppressed by who they identify with racially and socially.

A young Italian man came to my church for a short time. He had a preference for black women, but knew his family wouldn't approve, so he dated white women openly, and black women secretly. It reminded me of an account in Numbers 12:1–16, about Miriam and Aaron. The account tells us that God dealt severely with Miriam because I suppose she was the instigator. God caused her to become white as snow with leprosy. She didn't like black, so God made her very white!

This account tells me that God didn't have a problem with Moses marrying an Ethiopian woman; His concern was that His people would join themselves to heathen nations that would cause them to seek after other gods and learn their ways.

The Bible also says in Exodus 12:38 that Israel came out of Egypt with a mixed multitude, which this Ethiopian woman was a part of.

Your self-image

Your self-image is important in attraction because of interpersonal interactions. A person with a positive self-image will look confident, and be socially engaging. A person with a negative self-image will focus on what he or she believes to be character and physical flaws. They'll believe that everyone sees them as they see themselves, which causes social distancing. This can happen even when a person is attractive, and has achieved impressive things. Being comfortable in your own skin is important in building relationships, but young men and women with poor self-images, could look attractive, but perceive themselves as unattractive, which will affect their social life. What makes you attractive to someone may not be what you think, and you don't want to project your insecurities onto others. Consider a young man sitting alone comparing himself to all the other young men in the room. He believed they all saw themselves as handsome, and they were more physically fit than him. They wore clothes that were more fashionable than his, and he considered himself nerdy.

Out of nowhere, an attractive young woman, "one of the beautiful people," came and sat next to him. When she asked his name, without an answer he excused himself and made his exit for the bathroom. When he decided all was clear, he went to the corner of the room where he wouldn't be noticed by anyone.

The girls standing with the young woman who approached him didn't look his way, and he was fine with that. But what he didn't know, was that this pretty girl wasn't into pretty boys, and was always attracted to nerdy guys.

The girl's friends knew she had her eyes on him from the moment she noticed him, and when he rudely left her sitting alone, they were embarrassed for her, and upset with him. The young woman never attempted to approach him again, and the sad thing is, he didn't know that what may attract one person, may not be as appealing to someone else.

Consider the young foreign exchange student standing alone at a social mixer feeling out of place because she didn't speak the language well. What made things even more awkward, was that she was taller than most of the guys that were there. The fact that she was very attractive didn't help her confidence, because boys usually avoided girls they felt were too tall for them.

The young men who were checking her out were intimidated by her height, which prevented any of them from approaching her. But this one young man didn't seem to have any problem showing his interest in her, and started a conversation. The fact that she didn't have a command of the language, became a teaching moment for them both, and for the rest of the evening, they amused each other by learning how to say things in their different language. She felt very comfortable with him, and her height didn't seem to be a issue, so when he asked if he could see her again, she agreed. She found out later that he was always attracted to tall women, but taller women usually felt self-conscious with him. He loved the idea of having a tall woman at his side, and she loved that it didn't bother him that she was taller.

Attraction is universal and won't be bound by racial, cultural, or even language barriers. No matter what culture or society you're a part of, two people will find a way to show their attraction for one another. Attraction is the first step in the five steps to a good relationship, but it's important to find out about a person before committing to what pleases the eye. Also remember that attraction is subjective, and what may be attractive to you may not be as appealing to someone else; so don't allow the preferences of others to determine your choices. But people that are influenced by their cultural background, racial bias, and a poor self-image, can be prevented from approaching someone that attracts them.

CHAPTER 9

Can You Talk?

A word fitly spoken is like apples of gold in pictures of silver.
—Proverbs 25:11 KJV

As I said before, communication is the second step in the five steps to a good relationship, and the relationship builder. Communication is the thread that holds each step together because you can't build a relationship with someone you can't talk to.

Our initial attraction rests on appearance, but that can change after a conversation. A person's beliefs, opinions, and life views, may conflict with yours; but are overlooked when physical attraction becomes the most important thing.

Building a solid foundation

The ease in which two people can talk and exchange thoughts and feelings with one another, is what builds a solid foundation for a relationship. But when you connect on a sexual level, it causes ungenuine exchanges. The couple will relate to each other with sexual banter and believe their relationship is genuine because of that connection. They'll overlook personality differences because of a strong physical connection, and afterwards, have nothing more to offer.

Luke 6:45 (NKJV) says, "A good man out of the good treasure of his heart brings forth good, and evil man out of the evil treasure of his heart brings forth evil, for out of the abundance of the heart his mouth speaks."

Words are like verbal DNA painting a picture of the person doing the talking. What someone says tells you exactly who they are, if you're listening, and if you don't like what they're saying, you most likely won't build a healthy relationship with them. A person's character, values, and life beliefs, are more important than a physical attraction, but again, when physical attraction becomes the primary motivator in a relationship, it's hard to see who a person really is. There is also nonverbal communications that are more revealing than verbal communication, and when engaging a person, your ability to read those nonverbal communications becomes important.

How can you tell when someone's attracted to you? Did you know that if you're paying attention and know what to look for, you can tell?

Verbal communications have different tones and inflections that respond to what's being said, and a practiced person knows how to use them. But body language and facial expressions are involuntary and reflex, and even when practiced, they can betray the person speaking.

For example, a young man is engaging a girl in conversation. Her eyes wander, and she's easily distracted. Any observer would immediately notice that she wasn't interested in what the young man was saying, nor him. When we're paying attention, we'll take cues from facial expressions and body language, and a person would have to consciously control those things in order to conceal how they really feel, because body language and facial expressions are involuntary, and reflex.

Have you ever approached someone who was surprised to see you? They react according to how they feel about you. If they really didn't want to see you, you'll pick up on that the moment they notice you; but if they're glad about seeing you, it will be evident. It's the same with approaching someone who doesn't want to be bothered.

The way you should approach this second step is, "I hear what you say, but let's see what you do." Words are powerful, and relationships are established on what two people say to one another. A person's thoughts and feelings can be very conceptual, but what was said is confirmed when seen in practice. That's why it's important to give this second step time to prove itself.

CHAPTER 10

What Do You Have in Common?

*Do two walk together except they make an
appointment and have agreed?*
—Amos 3:3 AMPC

Socialization is the third step in the five steps to a good relationship. "What do you have in common in the people, places, and things you like?"

Most first encounters happen in a social atmosphere after meeting or seeing someone interesting. Maybe you were introduced through friends, and find that person is friendly, and you had a good conversation with them. If you're curious about where that encounter will lead, you should be taking mental notes, because the next time you're together, it may be a one-on-one date, which changes the dynamic from social to personal. This third step should help you decide if there's something more in the future for the both of you.

Two faces

Socialization provides an opportunity to see how someone conducts themselves socially and privately. We have two faces: a social face for social interactions, and a private face for personal interactions. Our private face is exclusive, but our public face is inclusive;

therefore, remember the story of Jekyll and Hyde, and never make the mistake of thinking you know someone until you know them socially and privately.

Dating

Dating is a social activity that provides you an experience in compatibility that helps you bond through shared activities. But here's a cautionary note; Until sex is taken off the table, your conversation and social activity will be in anticipation of what could happen at the end of the night. Therefore, dating should always be for enjoying each other's company, and never for sex.

In the early 1900s, dating was called courting. Courtship was a serious matter back then, and the young men that came calling did it under the watchful eye of either family or friends. The young men who came calling were called suitors, and the young women entertained as many suitors as they pleased. If the young woman was popular, she probably would have many suitors, and it was the young man's responsibility to compete to win her favor. Any displays of jealousy was considered distasteful, and could disqualify that young man as a suitor.

Each suitor was evaluated by the young woman's family, and if a man was found to be of questionable reputation, that also disqualified him from being a suitor. The family's reputation was held in high regard, and the family name was to be preserved and without scandal.

The young woman and her suitor was chaperoned by family members or close friends to social events, and private meetings were conducted in a common place under watchful eyes to assure that no boundaries were violated. Back then, young women weren't as accessible to men as they are today, and they didn't have the freedom of social movement without gaining a reputation. These things were in place to protect women from predatory men, but what was considered protecting a woman's reputation back then, has become an infringement on their privacy now. Today, young women have to be wiser than ever before when participating in social activities.

Courting gave young women the opportunity to evaluate each suitor without committing to them, until an engagement request was given and accepted. Today, unlike back then, there seems to be an unspoken rule, that if a man or woman is seeing someone, they can't entertain anyone else, even if there's no engagement request or promise of marriage.

Safeguards

Just like back then, friends and family still act as safeguards against wrong choices. The people closest to you can notice things you may miss, because they aren't emotionally invested as you are. Anyone that gets involved with you will directly or indirectly be involved with your friends and family. They are the people that will be happy to give insight and opinions based on their observations. What they say may not be what you want to hear, but whatever it is, will most likely be out of love for you.

A wrong choice can divide friends, destroy families, and cause emotional trauma for everyone involved, which makes it important to make the right partner choices, whether casual or significant.

Catfishing

I would like to end this chapter with catfishing. Attraction and communication can become one in socialization, to create a fictitious persona called a Cat fisher, because social media outlets are the way most people are communicating now. They're starting relationships online by picture posts, and connecting through messaging. Some are emotionally entangled with people they've never met, because they bonded with a picture, and are communicating with a stranger. The person that's catfished, is usually drawn to an image of someone, and bonds with them by online communication. The person doing the catfishing, uses that image as bait, and lures the person being catfished in with fictitious information.

The person being catfished forms an emotional bond in expectation that something real is developing, and invests in the assumption that the person they're communicating with really exists. Normally, we fall in love by spending time with someone we meet and get to know personally, but this relationship begins with an image and communications with the cat fisher. Someone being catfished develops those same feelings without ever meeting that person, and their intimacy is their social media connection.

Catfishing is more common than you think. About 23 percent of women, and 38 percent of men, have catfished someone. Dating apps are the number one place for catfishing, and account for nearly 40 percent of catfishing. There are five steps to a good relationship, and every step needs to be confirmed before moving to the next. Socialization should be a practical experience that's shared in the presence of a person after a good conversation, and not in their absence. Whenever you're searching dating sites and other social media, it pays to be overly cautious, because a sexy pic and the right conversation can bait you into unreal expectations. For every young man or woman who's ever been catfished, there was probably some friend or family member that threw up a red flag!

CHAPTER 11

How Serious Are You Willing to Get?

*One who is full loathes honey from the comb, but to
the hungry even what is bitter tastes sweet.*
—Proverbs 27:7 NIV

Commitment is the fourth step in the five steps to a good relationship. "How serious are you willing to get?" Are you ready to take your relationship to another level, or keep things status quo?

This fourth step is where most couples make an important decision, because every step from attraction to socialization was a proving ground up until this point. In this fourth step, you should consider if you want to get more serious, or if you're not sure because of a warning sign or red flag, you should wait.

When two people are right for each other, transitioning from one step to another should be easy. But if you're having difficulty in any of the steps, investing in the relationship may be a premature decision. It would be better to wait until you feel at peace about things.

A commitment determines the direction the relationship will take going forward, and every relationship should have a destination. The first three steps should have been working towards your decision, and this fourth step will determine what your relationship will look like going forward, or if it will even exist.

The investment

A committed relationship is an investment of time, emotions, and expectations into a future with someone. Time is a commodity, and who you spend your time on should be worth your investment. If you were investing money into something, you would expect a return on your investment, likewise, when you spend time on a person, you should expect a return on your time. The degree of your investment speaks to the value that person holds in your life, so make sure they're worth it. We prioritize our time around someone who's important to us by borrowing time from someone or something else to make time for them. But if that relationship ends, or you decide that it's no longer worth your investment, your loss is according to the amount of time you invested.

Premature commitments

There are people who stay in a relationship because they've invested too much time and resources to walk away. Obligating yourself to someone before you're sure if you're making the right decision is a premature commitment.

There are couples that move into an apartment, and bind themselves to a lease, and others purchase homes and aren't married, which makes the relationship transient! They've invested time and finance in someone that's not obligated to stay in their life. That's why a committed relationship should be preparation for marriage.

Couples that have been together for a long time become complacent. They adjust to the routine of their unchanging relationship, which makes marriage unnecessary. These are the couples that call each other husband and wife, and will tell you that they are married in the eyes of God. But when they split up, would God consider them divorced?

In the end, the emotional energy invested in a person you've been with for years is lost, and the hardest thing to walk away from, is someone you've invested so much time and emotion into, especially if there's children involved.

CHAPTER 12

Will You Marry Me?

*An excellent woman [one who is spiritual, capable, intelligent,
and virtuous], who is he who can find her? Her value is more
precious than jewels* and *her worth is far above rubies* or *pearls.*
—Proverbs 31:10 AMP

Marriage is the fifth and final step in the five steps to a good relationship. "Will you marry me?" Will you marry me, speaks to the value a person holds in your life and is the request for a return on the time, emotion, and expectations for a future with that person.

It shouldn't take years to decide if you want to marry someone, and if you're at that place in your relationship, you both should be on the same page. But whether you want to get married or not, your relationship still needs a firm foundation. Building a real relationship is like building a house, and you begin with a partner that wants to build with you.

Building your house

Again, every relationship should have a destination, and anyone in a relationship with you that doesn't see you in their future is transient.

So many young men and women that have matured through their experiences, look back and remember all the time they wasted on relationships that were going nowhere. But once you know what you're looking for in a partner, transient relationships won't satisfy you.

Evaluate every partner choice before you start to build a serious relationship with them. Survey the land and price the property to determine its value. These are metaphors, but it works toward a sound foundation. Believe that God wants you to be with someone who balances you and is suitable for you. The person you choose should be a complement to who you are, and both of you should help one another accomplish God's plan for your lives.

Unequally yoked

The Bible instructs us not to be unequally yoked with unbelievers. In 2 Corinthians 6:14 (KJV) it says, "Be ye not unequally yoked together with unbelievers, for what fellowship hath righteousness with unrighteousness? And what communion hath light with darkness?"

A person who professes Jesus Christ as Lord and Savior but chooses a partner who doesn't believe in Christ is unevenly yoked. This also applies to people of other belief systems who may believe in Jesus Christ, but not according to who the Bible says that He is. They may call Him a prophet, or a teacher, or a good man who did miracles, which isn't in line with scripture, and is uneven yoking.

Being yoked together with a person is joining with them, in the same way two oxen are joined at the neck for the purpose of plowing. They work in cooperation with one another as long as they're evenly yoked. But oxen that are unevenly yoked, will cause the stronger ox to work harder in order to keep the plowing on course. In other words, if the unbeliever's convictions are stronger than the Christian's that they're yoked with, that Christian will be pulled off course by that unbeliever.

That same yoking can be applied to a Christian joining themselves to a brother or sister in Christ, who isn't living right. If that Christian's relationship with Christ is only in profession and not in practice, joining with them can get you off course as fast as being yoked with an unbeliever. The Christian living for Christ has to have more influence over the Christian living out of fellowship, because being unevenly yoked can change the trajectory of your life.

Light and darkness

The Apostle Paul gives the metaphor of light contrasted with darkness as an example for a believer with an unbeliever. "Let me qualify what an unbeliever is, by saying they are persons that haven't received Jesus Christ as their Lord and Savior."

Light is visual energy that moves in a straight path. Darkness is the absence of light, and the two can't exist in the same place at the same time, unless something comes between the path of light to deviate it from its course.

The obstruction of light causes dimness and shadows, and the same thing happens to a believer who joins with an unbeliever. The unbeliever obstructs the believer's light and causes it to become dim and cast shadows.

Looking for your Soulmates

The term *soulmate* was written in a letter by a poet named Samuel Taylor Coleridge. He claimed in this letter, to be happy in married life, you must have a soulmate. For him, a successful marriage needed more than economic or social compatibility, it also required a spiritual connection.

Centuries before Coleridge, the Greek philosopher Plato, in his text "Symposium," wrote about the reasons behind the human yearning for a soulmate. Plato quotes the poet Aristophanes as saying, "All humans were once united with their other half, but Zeus split them apart out of fear and jealousy."

Aristophanes explains the transcendent experience of two soulmates reuniting in the following way. "When one of them meets with his other half, the actual half of himself, the pair are lost in an amazement of love, friendship, and intimacy. One will not be out of the other's sight, as I may say, even for a moment."

The idea of finding your soulmate shouldn't be so profound after that. When you have philosophers telling you how soulmates came into existence according to Greek mythology, and a poet giving you spiritual counseling about the nature of it, it's time to reevaluate the validity of what a soulmate is.

Do you really believe that God would create only one person in this whole world for you, and if so, what would be the chances of you finding that person? There's something in every one of us that anyone who's compatible with you will find suitable, and you have the benefit of choosing between many who have the same or similar qualities in different bodies. You just have to know what you're looking for.

Psalm 37:4–5 (KJV) says, "Delight thyself also in the Lord: and he shall give thee the desires of thine heart. Commit thy way unto the Lord; trust also in him; and he shall bring it to pass."

ABOUT THE AUTHOR

Pastor Reed Calaway was ordained into the ministry in 1994 under the leadership of Dr. Nathaniel Hayes and became the founder of Lifeline Ministries Inc., a nondenominational teaching ministry that received 501(c)(3) status as a nonprofit organization later that year. Rev. Calaway pastored in Connecticut for twelve years, and his teaching ministry aired on local cable stations and radio. He also became vital in launching other ministries as well. In 2005 Pastor Calaway moved to Florida and established Lifeline Ministries Orlando, which he pastored for five years. Most recently he's devoted himself to writing books compiled from manuscripts written during years of personal study and extensive research. Pastor Calaway's passion is to share the knowledge gained through his relationship with Jesus Christ, life experience, and pastoral counseling, with all who can learn from it.